SHE SPEAKS

THE WOMEN OF GREEK MYTHS
IN THEIR ♀WN WORDS

Honor Cargill-Martin

Illustrated by
Camelia Pham

MAGIC CAT 🐱 PUBLISHING

IN THIS BOOK, YOU WILL HEAR FROM . . .

PANDORA
PAGE 10

The first woman on Earth, who opened a jar of chaos onto the world

MEDUSA
PAGE 18

The powerful woman they called a monster

MEDEA
PAGE 26

The clever sorceress who helped Jason obtain the Golden Fleece

ATALANTA
PAGE 34

The strong huntress who fought in the Calydonian boar hunt

ARIADNE

The Cretan princess who
helped solve the Labyrinth
and stop the Minotaur

HELEN

The queen of Sparta who
found love on her own terms

PENTHESILEA

The Amazonian warrior
who led an army during
the Trojan War

CIRCE

The mighty witch-queen
who would do anything
to protect her island

WHAT HAPPENED NEXT?

Discover more about the original Greek myths

The Greek myths

ARE AMONG THE
GREATEST STORIES EVER TOLD.

They have all the ingredients needed to tell a great story: powerful magic, epic battles, enduring love, man-killing snake-hair . . . (yes, really!).

These myths were first written down around 2,700 years ago in the works of Greek poets Homer and Hesiod. But the stories themselves were being told long before then. They were passed down from one generation to the next through poetry, songs, and art. Each author had some artistic freedom to tweak parts of the story to make it more exciting or meaningful for their audience, so the stories that developed helped the Greeks understand their own, contemporary, world, as well as the world of the gods and goddesses. This way of telling stories means that no two surviving versions of a myth are ever completely the same—each one reflects the beliefs of the person who wrote it and the interests of the society they were writing for. The myths you'll read here are no exception—they aren't direct translations of Greek texts, they're retellings, designed to bring women right to the front of the action.

The myths in this book are told through words, but also (just as they would have been in ancient Greece) through art. The ancient texts don't tell us much about what individual characters were meant to have looked like, and when they do, they often disagree. The illustrations in this book take inspiration from ancient Greek art but they are designed most of all to capture the spirit of the women—after all, they *are* mythological and so you can imagine them looking however you like.

There are many versions of Greek myths, but what most have in common is that the women usually play supporting roles. That's because, for millennia, myths have been told from the point of view of gods and men—from Zeus to Hercules, Odysseus to Achilles. It's about time someone else got a say, and so the voices you'll hear in these pages are those of the women: Pandora, Medusa, Medea, Atalanta, Ariadne, Helen, Penthesilea, and Circe. Each gets the chance to tell her side of the story, from Medea's role in the myth of Jason and the Argonauts, to the part Ariadne played in the myth of Theseus and the Minotaur. They won't tell you their entire story (you'll have to turn to pages 68–73 for that), but they will tell you about some of the most important and dramatic moments in their lives. Most importantly, they finally get the chance to speak for themselves.

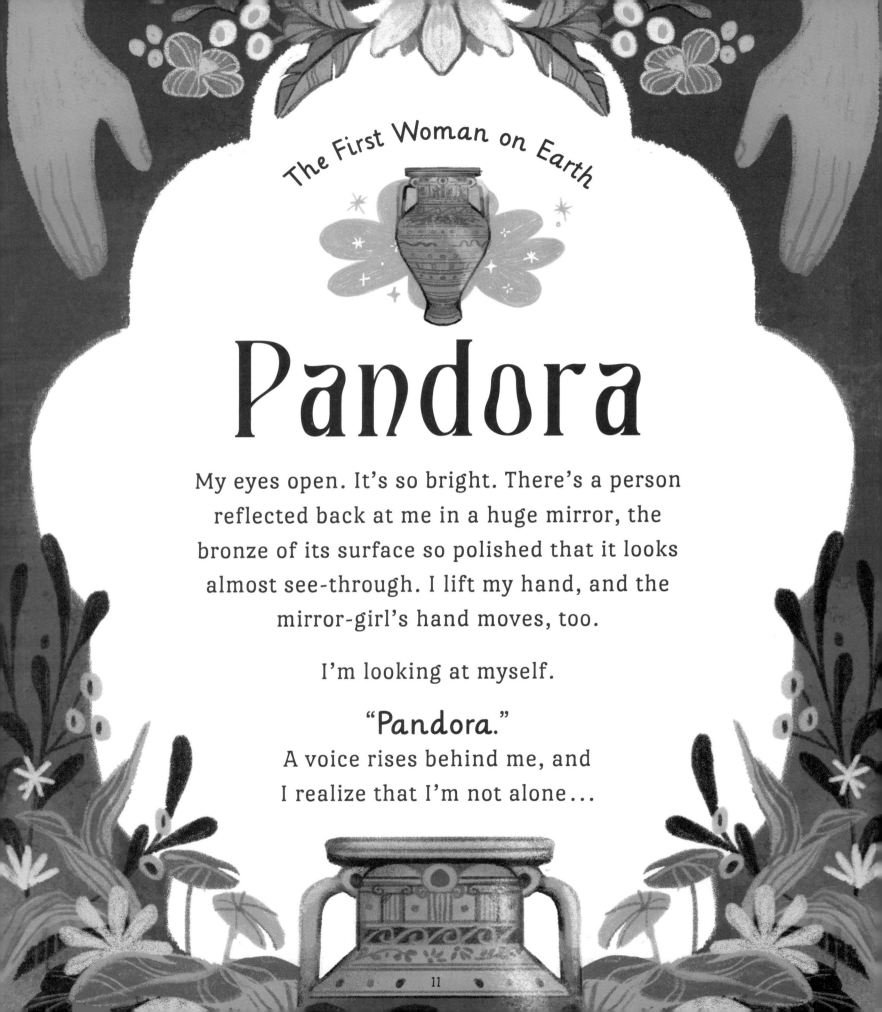

Pandora

My eyes open. It's so bright. There's a person reflected back at me in a huge mirror, the bronze of its surface so polished that it looks almost see-through. I lift my hand, and the mirror-girl's hand moves, too.

I'm looking at myself.

"Pandora."

A voice rises behind me, and I realize that I'm not alone...

I turn to see three figures, each reflected cloudily in the hall's golden floor. The man in the center—the one who spoke, I think—is older than the other two, with a long beard that forks in the center like a lightning bolt.

"It's a good name for the new creation, Zeus," says the woman next to him, looking me up and down with pale gray eyes. "Pandora—All-Gifted."

"Or All-*Giving*." The second man cuts in. He's slouched in an ebony chair near the door. He has wings growing out of the back of his boots and, every so often, one flutters angrily and he tells it to *shush*.

"Very clever, Hermes." The woman rolls her eyes.

"I wasn't saying you were wrong, Athena, just that the word could mean two things at once."

"Please," Zeus presses his fingers into his temples, "can we focus on the task at hand. I've explained to you both the next stage of the plan now that we've created the first woman—"

> "What do you mean the first woman?" I ask, the words forming easily on my tongue.

"What do you mean the first woman?" I ask, the words forming easily on my tongue. "And what *exactly* do you have planned?" The three of them stare as though they'd expected me to stand here and ask no questions at all.

No one answers me. Instead, Athena asks me to follow her, and I do. We walk out of the hall and into a marble courtyard. The sky above us swirls darkly. "It's from up there that Zeus gets his thunderbolts," Athena tells me. I watch her gown slip across the paving stones as I chase behind her. I notice that the hem is woven with delicate pictures of bloody battles.

"Where are we going?" I ask.

"To *my* palace," Athena replies.

I spend the next few weeks in Athena's halls. I learn that she's the goddess of all kinds of wisdom and skills—weaving and good-judgment, pottery and battle-strategy, and advice-giving. During the days, Athena teaches me to weave pictures into cloth; during the

evenings, Hermes teaches me the meanings of new words; during the nights, I lie in bed and wonder what Zeus meant by "plans."

Sometimes I look out of the windows and wonder about the world below, the valleys and forests I can see at the bottom of the mountain. Occasionally I think I notice the flicker of a bonfire or the speck of a boat skimming down one of the rivers—but I'm never quite sure.

One day, Athena wakes me early and says Zeus wants to see me.

"You're to marry," Zeus states as we cross the gold-paved hall toward him.

"Who?" I ask, "When? *Why*?"

"Today," he says, ignoring my other questions.

I open my mouth to argue, but then I start to think about it. This could be a chance to go down into the world and see what the fields and the rivers are like, to find out whether I'd only imagined the bonfires and the boats. The more I think about it, the more excited I become.

It's a rush to get ready. Athena has woven me a liquidy-gold dress and the other goddesses crowd around me too, slipping bracelets onto my wrists, winding necklaces around my neck, weaving herbs and flowers into my hair.

Finally, Athena fastens my veil in place with a golden crown—a gift from the metal-god Hephaestus—decorated with every type of earthly animal.

Back at Zeus' palace, ranks of horse-drawn chariots are pulled up in the courtyard ready to fly the gods to Earth. I'm riding in the first chariot with Zeus. Hermes is standing in front of us, the wings of his boots already fluttering, waiting to lead the procession. I lean forward. "What's my husband like?" I whisper.

"Kind, I think," Hermes considers, "but not as clever as you."

Then the gates of the courtyard swing open; the chariot speeds ahead and lifts off the ground. My knuckles turn white clutching the edge, until I realize the flight is so smooth that I don't have to hold on at all. I feel the rush of the air on my face, the cool dewiness as we fly through the clouds.

The wedding party is held in my husband's house—my new home. I try and get to know my new groom over the singing of the muses. His name is Epimetheus. He looks about my age with dark eyes and a wide smile. He smiles a lot, except when he tells me about his brother, Prometheus. Epimetheus says that his brother took pity on the men who were cold and unprotected and so he stole fire from Zeus and brought it down here to Earth. Apparently, Zeus was very angry and swore that he would get revenge on Prometheus, Epimetheus, and every single man on Earth. I say that I can't see why taking fire is that bad and Epimetheus nods, saying that our wedding must be a sign Zeus has finally forgiven him.

The chariot of the moon-goddess is high in the sky by the time the party is over. "Before we leave," Zeus shouts, kicking aside a dish to stand on top of the table, "I have a gift for the happy couple." He points to the most beautiful jar I have ever seen. It's almost as tall as me and covered in pictures: black-and-white painted figures against a red background.

My new life on Earth isn't bad—the world is beautiful and peaceful—but there are no other women here, only men, and it's not that *interesting*. Whenever I ask if we can explore, Epimetheus just looks nervous and says maybe and then we never do.

I do my best to enjoy myself, picking fruit from the orchard and weaving pictures of the tales Athena and Hermes told me. Whenever I pass the jar Zeus gave us for a wedding present, I try to trace the stories painted on it, but I'm sure they're not ones I've heard before.

The jar is shut with a lid and the more I think about it, the more I wonder if there's anything inside— and if there is, what it could be. I think it must be something very special or very interesting to be kept in a jar like that.

I'm not sure why Epimetheus and I have kept it closed for so long. After all, Zeus never exactly *ordered* us not to open it—he just gave it to us all sealed up and told us to put it in the hall. I start to wonder about what's inside every time I see the jar, and then even when I can't see it. I eat breakfast with Epimetheus and wonder. I spin thread and dye it deep-purple and wonder. I lie awake at night and wonder.

One day I can't stand it anymore. I clamber up onto a stool and push against the lid. It's heavy, but it's *not* sealed. It starts to give. I shove it again.

> I clamber up onto a stool and push against the lid ... The lid clatters to the floor and I'm thrown back.

The lid clatters to the floor and I'm thrown back.

There's a great rushing sound as streams of ashy-cloud shoot out of the jar, spiraling around the ceiling and then heading straight for the door. Each whirl of mist screeches out its name as it passes: "War!", "Hunger!", "Sickness!", "Hardship!".

I know that these are *Bad Things*. Horrible things that humans have never had to deal with before. And now they're out in the world. Because of *me*. I beat the stones with my hands. I realize I'm crying.

I stumble to my feet, trying to bat the misty whirls back with my arms, howling as they slip straight through my fingers. I have to do something. I try to feel for the lid in the darkness that has filled the room. Finally, I find it and heave it up, slamming it back over the top of the jar. As the room clears, I realize it's too late. The Bad Things have already escaped.

My mind flashes back to that first day on Olympus—how Zeus had said he had plans for me. Then I think back to our wedding day and what Epimetheus said to me about his brother. *This* must have been Zeus' plan all along: to use me to let all the badness out into the world, to make sure people went to war and got sick and got old ... all to punish mortals for Prometheus' theft of fire.

I stand up. I think I can hear something, a tiny whirring sound, still coming from inside the jar. I clamber back onto my stool, crack the lid and there, glowing just under the rim, I see it.

Cupping my hands, I gently, gently lift it out and I realize I know its name—it is Hope.

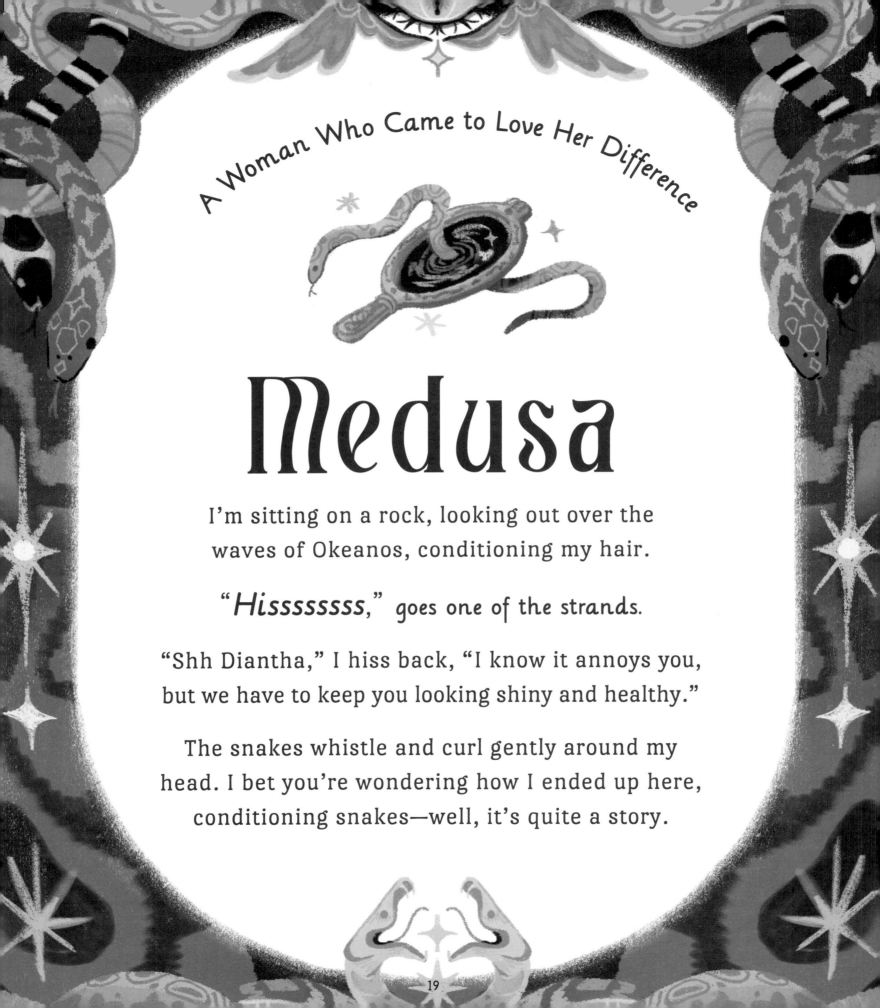

Medusa

I'm sitting on a rock, looking out over the waves of Okeanos, conditioning my hair.

"*Hissssssss*," goes one of the strands.

"Shh Diantha," I hiss back, "I know it annoys you, but we have to keep you looking shiny and healthy."

The snakes whistle and curl gently around my head. I bet you're wondering how I ended up here, conditioning snakes—well, it's quite a story.

I was born far away from here and grew up to be the most beautiful girl in my village. Everyone agreed that my hair was my crowning glory; it fell in long, shiny black curls all the way down my back. I didn't like the way people in the village stared at me—truthfully, I was lonely—and I spent most of my time down in the valley, near where the river met the sea. I was walking there when it happened. It had stormed the night before and mud was already caking the bottom of my dress. Mother would be furious when I got home, but I didn't care—I wanted to pick the spring flowers that were just starting to bloom.

I heard him before I saw him. A strange sound, somewhere between the clatter of hooves and the crashing of waves. A chariot was charging up the river toward me, drawn by horses with the tails of fish, shooting great sprays of water in its wake. I saw the driver's three-pronged trident and his billowing cloak and I realized, with a jolt of fear, who I was looking at. It was Poseidon, wrathful god of the sea—and if he was after me, it could only mean one thing; I was in the greatest of danger.

I ran as fast as I could, making for a sanctuary sacred to the goddess Athena which sat on top of the hill. I thought I'd be safe there, but Poseidon followed me inside. He towered over me, brandishing his trident, shouting threats. I started throwing things.

An ebony statuette, an alabaster offering bowl—anything to keep Poseidon away. Finally, I toppled a huge marble statue, sending it rolling right into the path of the god.

I think it was the deafening crash that alerted Athena—a sound so loud that it reverberated all the way up to Mount Olympus.

"What is the meaning of this?" she boomed, appearing next to her altar, tall and helmeted.

I found I couldn't speak at all. I was so scared that my tongue felt heavy and tied.

But Poseidon wasn't intimidated. He started telling Athena *all* about how he'd "discovered me trespassing in her temple" and "tried to stop me destroying her sacred property."

Athena's gray eyes sparked with anger. She raised her arms toward the heavens and muttered something under her breath. My head started to itch. I put my hand up and touched my head. I screamed as a clump of my own thick, dark, shiny hair fell away in my fingers. I put my hand up again and felt wriggling lumps all over my scalp. And then—*hissssss*—a snake emerged in the place of one of my old curls. *Hiiiisssssss*, another. And another. And another. Until my whole head was covered in curling, writhing serpents.

I put my hand
up again and
felt wriggling
lumps all over my
scalp. And then—
hissssss—a snake
emerged in the
place of one of my
old curls.

I started running. I didn't know where I was going. I couldn't go home—not like this. I ran until I couldn't run anymore and then I lay down to sleep in a cave cut into the hillside above a little town.

The sound of low voices twisting up the mountain path woke me up. I looked down and saw three men, heavily armed, marching up toward the cave. I could only catch snippets of their conversation: "probably dangerous," "kill the monster," "snakes for hair," "no match for us."

Panicking, I slipped back into the darkness of the cave and folded myself behind a rock, willing the hissing snakes to be a little quieter. I heard the clank of armor as the first of the men stepped into the cave. I peeked over the top of the rock. He saw me. He raised his sword high above his head. But then he stopped. His arm didn't move. He tried to run forward but his foot stopped mid-air. A cold whiteness began to spread across his skin. He started to scream but the sound withered away to nothing.

He raised his sword high above his head. But then he stopped. His arm didn't move.

The second man rushed toward his friend. He was only half inside the cave when he saw me. He stopped too, solidifying slowly in his tracks. The third man turned and ran. I could hear his screams in the distance as he hurtled back down the mountain toward the town.

I moved carefully out from behind the rock, not quite believing what I thought I saw. The men looked as though they'd *turned to stone*—but I had to be sure. I poked one in the stomach—nothing. I tickled the other under his arm— nothing. I threw a small rock at the top of the sword and it cracked into stony, shattered fragments.

I could hear a commotion rising from down in the valley. I'd have to leave this place immediately—the whole town would be after me soon. I stretched my shoulders and felt something heavy on my back. Two great gold wings had sprouted from my shoulder blades during the night. At first, I thought these must be another curse from the gods, designed to make me even more "monstrous." It was only once I'd taken flight that I began to think they

might have actually been a gift . . .

I flew for what felt like eons, over forests and deserts and rivers and mountains. Sometimes I'd dive low to watch people talking or eating or dancing. I wanted to join them, but I knew I couldn't—not now, not ever.

I kept flying, on past Atlas, the great Titan who holds up the sky, until I landed on a frosty ledge I assumed was uninhabited.

"Who goes there?" came a lisp from behind me. "Now, where did we put our eye?"

I twisted around to see three women, their skin white as ice, their hair silver. None of them had eyes, but one reached for a single eyeball, shining like a jewel on a golden tripod.

"N-no!" I stuttered, but it was too late. The eye had already been retrieved and the women were passing it between each other, each holding it up to take a good look at me.

They didn't seem to be turning to stone, but they were so pale that it might have been hard to tell.

"My, my," one of the women said, "if it isn't another Gorgon."

"Another Gorgon to be sure," her sister agreed passing the eye back to the first woman.

"Look, her snakes have just the same patterning as Sthenno's."

"Please," I begged. "Don't look at me!"

The first woman laughed. "Why not, my dear? Scared we'll turn to stone? No need to worry about us, darling, we're the immortal Graiai. Are you on your way to see your sisters?"

"I have sisters?" I stammered.

"Of course," the second woman rolled the eye she was holding, "the other gloriously snake-haired Gorgons."

"Wait," I couldn't keep up. "There's another woman like me?"

"There are *two*," the third woman smiled. "Fly on, just two days in that direction, and you'll find them."

So, I flew. Over the forests that grew in Atlas' shadow. Past the golden-appled gardens of the Hesperides, the sweet-singing nymphs of the evening. It was dusk on the second day before I saw the place the Graiai had talked of—a rocky strait lying right on the shore of Okeanos, the great river that encircles the whole world. And there they were—just as the Graiai had promised: two women, the Gorgons, with golden wings and glimmering snakes for hair.

And there they were—just as the Graiai had promised: two women, the Gorgons, with golden wings and glimmering snakes for hair.

The Gorgons began welcoming me before I'd even landed, rushing over, hugging me, calling me "sister," asking my name. I told them I was called Medusa, and they introduced themselves as Sthenno and Euryale.

Sthenno and Euryale had laid out a banquet for me in their palace of a cave. There was a whole platter of different dishes, and a side bowl filled with leaves and nuts for my hair to feast on.

We were hardly halfway through the second course when I started crying.

"I did something awful," I sobbed.

"What could you possibly have done?" Euryale weaved her arm around my shoulders.

"I-, I-, I turned two men to-to stone," I hiccuped.

"Hmmm," Sthenno passed me another cake slathered in honey, "and what were those men doing at the time?"

"They were coming to kill me. They said I was a monster."

"So, two men came to kill you and all you did in return was look at them?" Euryale repeated. "And yet you feel bad because they turned to stone?"

"You had to defend yourself, sister," Sthenno nodded gently, "those men would have killed you. Now," she twisted one of my snakes around her finger, "let's sort out this hair."

Sthenno and Euryale sat me in front of a shining bronze mirror, but I wouldn't even glance at my reflection. They started to untangle my mess of snakes and rub a hair mask made from olive oil, honey, and beeswax into the scales of each strand.

Finally, I looked at myself, and then I looked at Sthenno and Euryale. My sisters—with their golden wings and their heads of twisting, dancing snakes—looked so beautiful, and they looked just like me.

The Witch Who Got the Golden Fleece

Medea

The fire-breathing bulls have been tamed, the dragons' teeth have been planted, and the giant warriors are fighting amongst themselves.

I watch from a ledge above the flaming fields as Jason and his friends celebrate below. My father, King Aeetes, fumes beside me. I'm relieved Jason's safe, of course, but not surprised. How could I be?

Things have gone **exactly** how I planned.

A few days earlier I had been looking for my sister. Our palace is *huge* and a nightmare to find people in. It was built for my father—Aeetes, son of the sun-god Helios and ruler of Colchis, the land that lies at the eastern edge of Earth—by Hephaestus, god of craftsmen. I'd walked through countless courtyards, climbing my way up through the towers that soar above the city below, and I was rounding the corner into the thousandth hall when I bumped into him.

He looked like no one I'd ever seen before. I've always been the kind of girl who knows what she wants, and I knew I wanted this man to be my husband.

> I've always been the kind of girl who knows what she wants, and I knew I wanted this man to be my husband.

That night my father laid out a feast for the stranger. I said nothing all dinner—instead, I watched and listened and planned.

The stranger said that his name was Jason and that he had come from the far-off land of Greece. His uncle had stolen his rightful place on the throne of Iolcus, but had promised to give him back his kingdom if he traveled to Colchis and brought back the Golden Fleece. I watched my father's expression darken.

The Golden Fleece is no *ordinary* sheepskin—it is a sacred symbol of power. Every curl of its wool shines with royal gold. It is one of my father's most prized possessions and he has gone to great lengths to protect it. The Fleece hangs high in a grove of trees sacred to the war-god Ares.

> The Golden Fleece is no *ordinary* sheepskin ... every curl of its wool shines with royal gold.

It is guarded night and day by a serpent bigger than a ship, whose watchful gray eyes never close, protecting this sign of authority and kingship.

I know my father cares about power more than anything else—there was no way he was going to give Jason the Fleece without a fight.

"I'll give you the Fleece," my father began, "if you just do one or two very simple tasks for me first. There's a field on the plain of Ares that I want planted. You'll have to yoke my oxen and plow it with the seeds I give you. Can you do that?"

"Of course." Jason nodded eagerly. *He had no idea what he was in for*, I thought.

"The bulls breathe fire," my father went on. Jason was starting to look less confident. "And the seeds are dragons' teeth. When they're planted, fully grown, armed warriors will spring from the ground to try and kill you. If you survive that, *then* I'll give you the Golden Fleece. Do we have a deal?"

"Um, y-yes?" Jason was shaking and I knew then that I had to help him. Without my magic, those tasks would mean certain death . . . and besides, stealing the Golden Fleece sounded like just the sort of adventure I'd been looking for.

I hardly slept that night. I rooted through my witchcraft books and boxes of ingredients, and I waited for the dawn. As soon as my grandfather, the sun, began to rise, I gathered my twelve ladies-in-waiting and harnessed my chariot horses. We sped through the city streets and out across the plains to the tree-shaded sanctuary of Hecate.

Hecate, with her two flaming torches and her huge black dog, is the goddess of witchcraft, and I, like my aunt Circe before me, am her priestess. I look after the sanctuary

and see that her sacrifices and rituals are performed to perfection. In return, she has granted me the most powerful gift a woman can possess—*knowledge*.

She has granted me the most powerful gift a woman can possess—*knowledge*.

I'd sent word to Jason to meet me here at the start of the third hour, but I had a potion to make before he arrived.

There's only one ingredient that can make a man invincible. Meadow saffron. Little purple flowers, growing on twin stems that are two feet tall, filled with fire-orange pollen. The flowers first grew from drops of Prometheus' blood, which fell when he was punished by Zeus for stealing fire, and the juice that comes from their roots is the darkest of reds. In the wrong hands it can be deadly, but in the right ones it can save a man's life.

I untied my ingredients box and pulled out a seashell—the deep red of the meadow saffron extract now glowing in its center. A few drops would be all that were needed, mixed with the smoothest olive oil and poured into an ordinary looking flask.

Jason arrived bang on the third hour. He'd come alone, as I had told him to, and he looked even more handsome than he had the night before. We sat in the shade for a while and talked. He spoke about how beautiful his hometown was and told me the story of a girl named Ariadne who saved a hero called Theseus and how she was honored by the gods forever more. Then he begged me, in the names of Hecate and Zeus, to save his life.

"I can help you," I said, "but you must to do *exactly* as I tell you. One slip up and the whole charm will fail."

"I can help you," I said, "but you must do *exactly* as I tell you. One slip up, and the whole charm will fail."

"I swear."

"Get up at midnight tonight, bathe in the river and dress in clothes of the darkest navy-blue. Walk until you're far away from where you and your friends have camped and dig a

hole. Build a bonfire above the pit and make a sacrifice to my goddess Hecate, sweetening it with a few drops of honey. Then turn and walk away. Let nothing—not the sound of footsteps, not the barking of dogs—make you turn back around and look at that bonfire again. At the first light of dawn cover your whole body with this potion. From then on, until nightfall nothing will be able to harm you. Still, you'll have to work fast. The warriors that grow from the dragons' teeth are giant and fearsome but they're also very easily distracted. Throw a stone into their midst and they'll fight over it rather than attacking you. That way you can focus on getting the field plowed before the sun sets and the charm wears off."

The next day, my father assembled the whole Colchian court on a ridge overlooking the field of Ares. I smirked a little as I listened to them crowing about how the "tasks were impossible" and there was "no way that Jason could possibly survive." I knew my father would never suspect me. He never listened to me and my sister—he definitely wouldn't believe that I might be able to outwit him.

The bulls stamped their bronze hooves and snorted out plumes of fire as Jason approached. They roared and pummeled him with their horns, but they couldn't hurt him. My charms had made him stronger than strong, and he harnessed them easily to the plow. The whole court was quiet now.

My father was dumbstruck. He looked angry when Jason planted the dragons' teeth seeds, angrier still when he threw a rock into the midst of the warriors that sprung up from the ground and even angrier when he slew them all one by one.

It was nearly sunset when Jason returned, his tasks finally completed.

Back at the palace that night, my father rages at his advisors. "I don't care that he finished the tasks I set. The Golden Fleece is *mine*, and I will kill him before I give it to him." I have to warn Jason.

"The Golden Fleece is *mine*," my father raged, "and I will kill him before I give it to him!"

I slip from the palace, whispering spells to unbolt door after door, and run, barefoot, through the city, over the fields and down to where Jason's boat is moored on the river. Panting, I tell him everything and propose a new plan: we'll have to steal the Fleece for ourselves.

Jason follows me as I lead him to the sacred grove where the Fleece hangs, floating like a golden cloud at sunset. Curled around the base of the tree is the great serpent. Always watching for thieves, it never sleeps, in fact, it never even blinks.

"Stay back," I whisper to Jason.

The serpent raises its head and lets out a long shuddering hiss as I creep forward. There's only one spell I can think of and I have no idea if it will work. I begin to chant a soft, sweet lullaby and the serpent's head begins to sway. Then, reaching into the folds of my dress, I draw out a potion—juniper berries and water from the Lethe, the river of oblivion which flows through the underworld—and sprinkle it over the serpent's eyes. His eyelids flicker for a minute, then shut. His head hits the ground with a thud and the earth seems to shake with a huge snore.

"Quick!" I mouth, motioning to Jason to grab the Fleece, stroking the head of the sleeping serpent until he's unhooked it from the tree and slung it over his back.

Then we run. Out of the grove, over the hills, down the riverbank. Until we reach the ship. Jason and I swing ourselves on board just as the crew raise the anchor and untie the ropes. The sails unfurl with a cracking sound and then we're off—headed for Greece.

Jason hauls himself onto the upper deck and addresses the crew: "We have the Golden Fleece because of Medea's cleverness. She has saved all of Greece—and every one of you!"

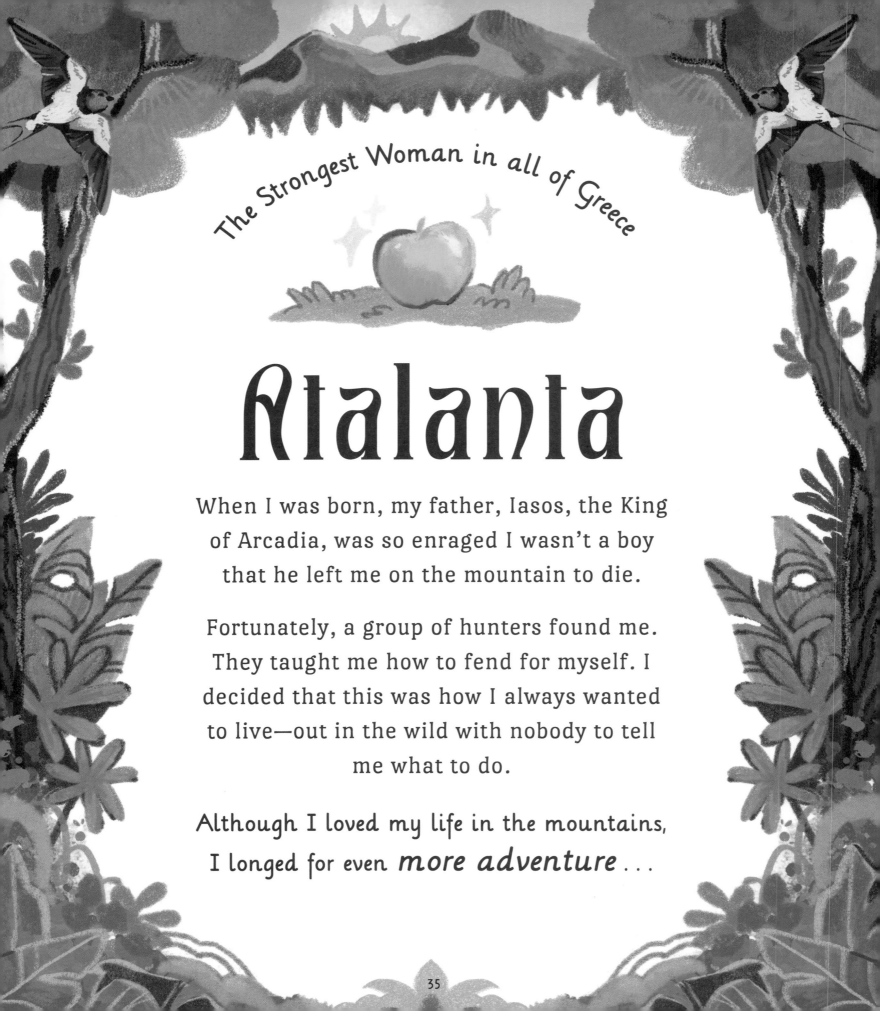

The Strongest Woman in all of Greece

Atalanta

When I was born, my father, Iasos, the King of Arcadia, was so enraged I wasn't a boy that he left me on the mountain to die.

Fortunately, a group of hunters found me. They taught me how to fend for myself. I decided that this was how I always wanted to live—out in the wild with nobody to tell me what to do.

Although I loved my life in the mountains, I longed for even *more adventure* . . .

It was the end of summer when I first started to hear whispers of a monstrous boar roaming Calydon. The travelers and hunters that passed through my woods told tales of a mighty animal that had been sent by Artemis, the goddess of

hunting, to punish the King of Calydon for failing to make offerings in her honor. They said it was far bigger and more fearsome than *any* boar *any* man had *ever* seen before. It was ravaging the whole country, they claimed, destroying the crops and terrorizing the people. At first, I thought they were exaggerating, but then a messenger arrived.

"Any heroes around here?" he asked.

"Who wants to know?" I replied.

"The King of Calydon. He's assembling the greatest hunting party on Earth, made up of all the greatest huntsmen and heroes of Greece. They're going to kill the Calydonian Boar."

> "The King of Calydon. He's assembling the greatest hunting party on earth, made up of all the greatest huntsmen and heroes of Greece. They're going to kill the Calydonian Boar."

"I'll go," I said, grabbing my cloak.

"What?"

"I said *I'll* go."

"But- but- " the messenger stammered, "you're a— "

"A what?"

"A woman!"

"*AND?*"

The messenger still looked dubious, so I pulled out my bow and shot an arrow straight through his traveling cap. "Well," he said, prizing his cap down from where the arrow had pinned it to a tree trunk, "I suppose you had better come with me."

As we passed through the mountains of Aetolia toward Calydon, I realized that all the stories had been true. Trees and bushes had been trampled, crops had been dug up, men

and animals had been killed. The villagers huddled in their doorways—their animals locked in barns, their children kept inside—as we passed.

Nor had the messenger been exaggerating when he said that the king was gathering the greatest hunting party ever seen. His hall was packed with young champions sent from cities across the Greek world. They were talking tactics, counting their arrows and sharpening their spears, but they all turned when I walked in.

There were whispers and then shouts—some of the men couldn't stand the idea of hunting alongside a woman.

But Meleager, the leader of the hunt, was having none of it. He knew a great hunter when he saw one.

"She hunts alongside us," he declared, "and that's the end of it."

We assembled at daybreak the next morning with our packs of hunting dogs and our weapons. The hunting horn sounded and we were off, into the thickly forested hills in search of the boar. It didn't take us long to find the monster's tracks—huge hoof-marks clomping through the mud. We began to follow them up mountains, into valleys, along rivers, and through caves.

We heard a thunderous ROAR, and there it was . . . The biggest boar I'd ever seen, with

eyes that burned like hot coals, sharp spikes of hair and foam dripping from its tusks. We raised a cry, spread our nets and grabbed our weapons.

The boar charged!

Some of the men threw spears and missed; one jumped forward only to be impaled on the boar's tusks. I waited and watched for the perfect moment.

I raised my bow, pulled back the string, and let an arrow fly. It whistled through the air—right into the boar's neck.

"Atalanta has drawn first blood!" shouted Meleager. "Show some respect for her courage."

> I raised my bow, pulled back the string, and let an arrow fly.

We feasted that night at the palace. It was Meleager who finished the job I started and killed the boar, so its body was given to him as a prize. He split the meat among the whole hunting party—but he awarded *me* the tusks and the great bristling boar skin. It was the most important prize of all. Seeing a woman win it outraged some of the men. They started to threaten me—demanding I hand over the tusks and boar-skin to them. Meleager became horrified at how his soldiers were acting. He picked up his sword and killed them on the spot. After all, I *had* won the prize fair and square.

My victory over the Calydonian boar made me famous all throughout Greece. That's how my father found out I was alive. He begged me to come back and live with him and my family. I thought about it and agreed to return.

At first things were going well—but then he started trying to tell me what to do. Most of all he wanted me to get married. He went on and on about it, saying that it was my "job as a woman." *As if.* I'd already promised myself that I would never marry—and my job was being the greatest hunter in all of Greece.

I decided to offer my father a deal: I would marry any man who could beat me in a race. He was over the moon, but I wasn't worried; I'd met the greatest heroes in the world, and there wasn't a single one who could run as fast as me.

Soon, men were pouring in from all over Greece, ready to compete for my hand in marriage. It went the same way every time. The men would sit at dinner the night before the race and boast: "I'm the fastest man in my whole city!," "faster than anyone who's ever lived!," "there's no way I could *ever* be beaten by a woman!" And then, the next morning, we'd race . . . and I'd beat them.

I decided to offer my father a deal: I would marry any man who could beat me in a race.

The same story repeated itself over and over, until one day a man named Hippomenes, descended from the sea-god Neptune, arrived. This time, things were different from the start. First of all, I actually *liked* talking to him. He was funny, he loved hunting, and he told me how much he respected my strength and speed. When I asked if he thought he would be able to beat me in the race the next day, he said "No!" And then more quietly

he added, "*at least not on my own!*" It was weird—I *almost* found myself wishing that Hippomenes would win the race so that we'd have to get married . . . but there was no way I was going to lose a race on purpose.

When I woke the next morning, I could hear the crowds forming down by the track.

"Ready to lose?" I asked Hippomenes as we reached the starting line.

"Never readier," he smiled.

The trumpet sounded, and we were off!

At first, I took the lead easily—*this will be easy*, I thought—but Hippomenes gained on me as we rounded the first corner. He was fast, I'll give him that. I sped up; there was no way he'd be able to beat me but at least it looked like he was going to give me a proper race.

Then something glinted at the corner of my vision. It flashed bright gold as it shot past me into the trees. I knew I shouldn't follow it, but I also knew I'd be able to make up whatever time I wasted by just running a tiny bit faster. I veered off the track and into the woods.

It didn't take long for me to catch it. A solid golden apple! In all my years of hunting, this was the shiniest, brightest, most beautiful thing I'd ever caught and it felt heavy and smooth in my hands. I tucked the apple into my tunic and raced back onto the track.

This time I saw Hippomenes do it. Just as I was overtaking him, he pulled out a second golden apple and threw it into my path. Again, I dashed into the woods and caught it.

Hippomenes had really taken the lead this time, but still, I soon overtook him.

We were near the finish line now, and he was right behind me. I got ready to sprint. Again, there went that flash of glittering gold. I *knew* I shouldn't—but I couldn't resist . . . I hurtled back out of the woods, clutching the apple, just in time to see Hippomenes crossing the finish line!

"You CHEAT!" I screamed, storming off in the direction of the palace. Hippomenes had tricked me!

"Atalanta!" he shouted after me, but I didn't turn around. "*Atalanta!*"

I paused.

"Atalanta, I'm sorry," Hippomenes said. "I knew I'd never be able to beat you on my own."

"*Obviously* not." But I was intrigued. "So how did you do it?" I asked.

"I prayed to the goddess Aphrodite. She could see how much I loved you and she thought you might fall in love with me too. She gave me the apples, pure gold and enchanted with a divine love spell, to distract you."

"*Aphrodite?* As in, the goddess of love?" I asked. I was laughing now—I couldn't help it—it was so ridiculous.

"Yes." Hippomenes hung his head.

I looked at him and was surprised by how happy I felt. I was glad he'd done it. Still, I wanted him to sweat a little.

After a brief pause, he spoke again. "I'm sorry I lied. But I do love you, and hope you love me too. If you agree to marry me, we can go hunting every day, and I'll never, ever, ever forget the fact that you're faster than I am."

"Do you promise?"

"I promise."

"Then my answer is yes, I'll marry you."

The Cretan Princess Who Cracked the Labyrinth

Ariadne

My hands shake a little as I steal along
the passages of my father's palace.

I can feel the long red spool of thread
hidden inside the folds of my gown.
I told my mother I was spinning
it to weave a new veil, but really

I'm going to use it to catch
a monster . . .

My family, royal though it is, has its fair share of secrets. All families do, I suppose, but ours is bigger and more monstrous than most.

My father, King Minos, is very rich, very powerful, and sometimes very careless. Once, years ago, he was foolish enough to break a promise he'd made to Poseidon, god of the wild seas that surround our island. Poseidon was so angry that he cursed our family, and my mother, Pasiphae, gave birth to something nobody had ever seen before—it was a monster that had the body of a man but the head of a bull. People called it the Minotaur.

It was a monster that had the body of a man but the head of a bull. People called it the Minotaur.

My father was scared and ashamed. He just wanted the problem of the Minotaur to disappear. So he called on Daedalus—the cleverest artist and inventor in the world—to build a prison for the Minotaur right beneath our palace, one from which it would be impossible to escape.

The Minotaur was too strong to be kept in by locked doors and iron bars alone. Instead, Daedalus built a maze with so many twisting turns and dark dead ends that, once inside, it was impossible to find your way out. He called it the Labyrinth.

My father left the Minotaur in the center of Labyrinth and tried to forget about him. It didn't work. The Minotaur got hungrier and angrier until the stone floors of the palace shook with his bellowing. We offered him every type of food but he wouldn't touch any of it. Poseidon's real curse was that the creature would only eat people.

My father couldn't bear to feed his own people to the Minotaur so he invaded the land

of Attica and besieged the city of Athens until they agreed to send him seven young men and seven young women every nine years as food for the monster. Two shipments had come already: the first I was too young to remember, when the second arrived I was too young to understand what was happening until it was too late.

It was only after half of the Athenians had been forced into the endless maze and not a single one had returned that I realized—these guests had been brought here as food for the Minotaur. How could my father have planned this? How could all these grown-ups have known what was going to happen and yet have done nothing to stop it? I vowed then that when the next boat arrived from Athens in nine years' time I would stop the sacrifices for good. For years, I planned and plotted so that by the time the black-sailed Athenian ship appeared on the horizon, I was ready.

I vowed then that when the next boat arrived from Athens in nine years' time I would stop the sacrifices for good.

So here I am, all those years later, taking my dutiful place on the shore beside my father as he inspects the shivering Athenians and blesses them as sacrifices to Poseidon. I inspect them too: looking for the strongest and most defiant person. I need an accomplice on the inside. One person stands out. His name is Theseus. He looks taller and stronger than the others—he needs to be if he is to have any chance against the Minotaur—and there is a glint of fearlessness in his eyes. He will make the perfect ally.

45

That afternoon, I decide to talk to him, stealing down the stairs to the dungeons of my father's palace. The guard is snoring on his stool.

"Theseus," I whisper through the bars.

"I saw you on the shore." He looks at me through narrowed eyes. "You're Minos' daughter."

"Yes," I admit, "but I'm here to help you. I don't believe you plan to go down without a fight. I can see it in your eyes."

He looks at me warily, like he's scared I'm my father's spy. "You're right," he says slowly, "I intend to volunteer to be the first sacrifice then to fight the monster to the death in the hope that I might be able to save my people."

"Even if you defeat the Minotaur tomorrow," I whisper, "you'll die trapped in the Labyrinth. I've brought you a solution." I fish the spool of thread out from my gown. "Tie the end of this thread to the gate and let it unravel as you walk. Find the Minotaur—it won't be hard, you can hear him a mile off—and put up the fight of your life. If by some miracle you win, you can use the thread to retrace your steps and find your way back to the entrance."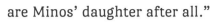

"Why would you do this?" Theseus asks.

"I can't sit by and watch innocent people die." I slip the spool of thread between the bars for

him to take.

"But how can I know I can trust you? You are Minos' daughter after all."

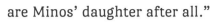

"You can't," I shrug. "But it's your only chance at survival."

Theseus takes the thread—he knows what I'm saying is true. "Thank you," he says and begins to turn away.

"Wait!" I grab his arm. "There's something I ask in return. I can't stay here, especially not now I've double-crossed my father. I need to escape."

He nods. "It's a deal. Wait for me by the entrance.

If I make it out alive, we can sail straight for Athens."

My father throws a feast the next day, to mark the first of this year's sacrifices to the Minotaur. Theseus, it is announced, has volunteered to go first. There's music and dancing. I don't know how these people can celebrate but I thank the gods that they're distracted.

I slip out, swiping a set of palace keys from a bored-looking guard on my way past. The sound of music grows quieter and the roars of the Minotaur grow louder as I steal down ramps and ladders to reach the gates of the Labyrinth. I hear the Minotaur bellow and Theseus shout. Then there's a howl, a groan, and a loud thud. I hold my breath until, finally, Theseus reappears, covered in dirt and blood . . . and clutching my ball of thread.

I grab his hand and pull him toward the cells where the rest of the Athenians have been locked away. "Wait here," I say as we reach the corner, chucking him the bunch of stolen keys, "I'll distract the guard—you sneak past me and unlock the rest of the prisoners. That way we *all* get out of this alive."

I prattle on and on to the guard about the weather and the festival of Poseidon until I've counted out thirteen soft clinks: the sound of all the thirteen remaining prisoners being unlocked. Then I *run*.

I run through the maze of palace corridors—Theseus and the Athenians following my lead—out through the courtyards and down the terraces, across the fields and the forests, down the cliff path and along the pier. One by one, we leap onto the deck of the Athenian ship. I'm still panting as the sails unfurl and the ship rocks into motion, but I don't feel tired.

A monster has been defeated, and fourteen innocent lives have been saved—because of me.

A Woman Whose Worth is More Than Her Beauty

Helen

People have always stared at me.

They tell me I'm the demi-god daughter of Zeus, that I was hatched from a swan egg, and that I'm the most beautiful woman in the world.

None of that matters to me. I don't want to be looked at; I want to be loved. The kind of love I'd choose for myself.

The kind I'd start **a war** for.

The time came when my stepfather, King Tyndareus of Sparta, decided it was time for me to marry. Suitors flooded in from all corners of Greece, each bringing great trains of gifts: bronze cauldrons, herds of animals, hoards of gold. They all made long speeches about "love," but I knew what they really wanted me for: my beauty and my wealth. Sparta was my inheritance, and I had the power to make whoever I married its king. They all stared at my face, my hair and my body, but none of them cared about my other qualities. I'm clever, passionate and I can make a speech to rival any man, but these suitors just wanted me to look beautiful. And most devasting of all—to be silent.

But as more and more men arrived, my stepfather began to panic. He was scared that by choosing one he would anger all the rest, and that when I was married, the other suitors would try to steal me away from my husband and from Sparta. So, he made a plan: any man who wished to compete for my hand had to sign a pact promising that if anyone ever tried to take me away from my future husband, they'd be willing to go to war to bring me back to him. The pact protected King Tyndareus and my husband . . . but it paid no heed to what I might want.

In the end, it was decided that I was to marry a man named Menelaus. He hadn't even come to propose to me in person; he'd sent his brother Agamemnon to speak on his behalf. Menelaus wanted to marry me because he'd heard tales of my exceptional beauty, and Tyndareus accepted his offer because he was the richest man in the whole of Greece. Nobody cared how I felt. It's hard to fall in love with someone you've never met, and it's even harder to believe they truly love you.

It's hard to fall in love with someone you've never met, and it's even harder to believe they truly love you.

50

When Menelaus heard he'd been chosen, he rushed to Sparta to marry me, and when Tyndareus died, we ruled together as king and queen. Menelaus wasn't a bad man but we had nothing in common. I loved poetry, stories, hunting, and singing; he loved going to war, preparing for war, and talking about wars he'd gone to. I couldn't help but think that he was happier that he'd married the "Most Beautiful Woman in the World" than that he'd married *me*.

I was Helen, daughter of Zeus, the most ambitious and restless of all the gods, and here I was, living in the town I'd grown up in, married to a man my stepfather had chosen for me. I wasn't exactly unhappy, but I hardly ever felt *alive*.

"Helen! Helen!" My best friends Clymene and Aethra rushed into my room one morning. "There's word in the town that a fleet of strange ships are sailing into port."

I threw on a veil, harnessed a chariot, and set out to see for myself. Clymene, Aethra, and I clutched each other's hands as we pushed through the heaving crowds of the harbor's marketplace. My friends were right; these boats certainly did not come from any part of Greece. They were made of shining oak and pinewood, their sterns decorated with brightly-colored paintings of the gods. The largest of the ships had a gold sculpture fixed to its prow: Aphrodite, goddess of love, and her son Eros. Standing on the deck behind the statue was the most beautiful man I'd ever seen. His skin shone, his hair curled around his face, but most interesting of all was his gaze—it seemed to shoot right through you.

I didn't have to wait long to discover who he was.

"We have a guest coming to dinner this evening, my dear," Menelaus announced when I returned home. "Man by the name of Paris. Prince of some place called Troy. Far off country in the south . . . no, the north . . . maybe the west? Barbarians if you ask me, but he could be useful. *Politically,* you understand." Menelaus told me Paris was here on some sort of "complicated" diplomatic mission and refused to explain any further. He said it was men's business, but I'm certain he just didn't understand it himself.

The dinner was the best night of my life. I had never met someone like Paris of Troy. He asked me question after question and told me stories of the wonders of his homeland which, it turned out, was in the *east.*

"Troy seems an endless land, stretching from the snow-topped mountains to the sea," he said. "It's a world of gleaming temples, turreted cities and terraced palaces. There are crowds like you've never seen before, marketplaces piled with silks and gold and gems, air that smells like smoke and cinnamon."

The next morning Menelaus left for Crete. "Business, business!" he kept saying. "You don't need to worry your pretty head about it. Just stay here, look after the house and make sure our guest is well taken care of."

Over the days that followed, Paris and I got to know each other better. Every dinner, I watched him watching me. Whenever I took a sip of wine, he would raise the cup to his lips and drink from the same spot. I was used to men looking at me, but this felt different; I felt a feeling I'd never felt for myself before. I was in love.

Menelaus has been away for weeks now. During our days Paris and I walk through the olive groves that shade the hills around Sparta; he tells me stories about his homeland and childhood, and I tell him stories about mine. In the evenings we feast on wild cherries

> The dinner was the best night of my life. I had never met someone like Paris of Troy.

and honey cakes, and he sings me songs about the loves of the gods.

One night I pluck up the courage to ask Paris what had really brought him to Sparta. "As Queen Helen of Sparta," I begin in the haughtiest voice I can muster, "I demand to know the nature of your diplomatic business with my husband."

"What?!" Paris laughs. "My business with your husband? Helen, I came to Sparta to meet you. I wanted to know if the tales told of you were true."

"And were they?"

"No. You are far more interesting and far lovelier than they said. I love you, Helen, and—I know this sounds wild—but if you love me too, let's run away together. If you come to Troy, I will worship you and give you treasures beyond—"

I stop him. "I have treasure enough of my own ... but I love you too, Paris." I can hardly believe I've said it, but now I have there's no going back. "I want to come to Troy with you."

While Paris readies the ships to sail, I write a letter to Menelaeus. I tell him that I'm leaving with Paris out of love and my own free will. Then I remind him that Aphrodite, goddess of love, is the most powerful goddess of all—even my own father Zeus cannot disobey her commands. Finally, I beg him not to follow me. I know there's a risk that he could call in the oath my stepfather Tyndareus made my suitors sign and muster a thousand-ship fleet to pursue me and Paris. I pray he won't, but now it lies in the lap of the gods.

After all, if men are going to fight over me, I should at least get to choose which side I'm on.

The Queen of Warrior Women

Penthesilea

Tomorrow, at dawn, I will lead my
comrades into battle against the Greeks.
They're fearsome warriors, led by powerful
Agamemnon, cunning Odysseus, and
invincible Achilles, but I'm not scared of them.

I am the daughter of Ares, god of war,
and queen of the Amazon tribe
of warrior women.

I was born to *fight*.

The Amazons and I live on the plains of Thermodon. Our society is made up only of women; there are no men at all. Here, it's women who make the decisions, women who hunt for our food, and, most importantly, women who fight our wars. I'm told that in other far-off lands women are believed to be weaker than men—I never heard nonsense like that growing up among the Amazons.

Amazons start our training young and that's how we become true masters at the art of war. We learn to run and to ride, to shoot a bow and arrow, to throw a spear and hunt wild animals, and, finally, to fight in one-to-one combat with swords and battle axes. The problem is that when you're young, you don't always understand how dangerous those things can really be. I was only a teenager when my sister, Hippolyte, and I were sent out on a deer hunt. We were working together—speeding through the trees and cornering the animal—when I finally got the deer in my sights. Patience has never been one of my virtues and I was caught up in the moment, desperate to prove my prowess. I didn't stop to think before I hurled my spear. The weapon shot through the air, but the deer leaped away. Standing where the deer had been was Hippolyte, but it was too late—my spear hurtled straight toward her and hit her.

> Here, it's women who make the decisions, women who hunt for our food, and, most importantly women who fight our wars.

When I realized Hippolyte was dead, I was so overcome with grief and shame that I fled Thermodon and began to wander the world. Even though Hippolyte's death had been an accident, the gods were enraged. I needed to undergo a ritual of purification—a series of ceremonies that would prove to the gods and my sister's spirit just how sorry I was. But purification is a complicated ritual and I had to find a priest wise and powerful enough to perform it. The only one I'd heard of was Priam, king of the city of Troy, and so I set out to seek him.

The journey was long and hard, but I was shocked by how kind King Priam was to me when I arrived, and even more shocked that he continued being kind to me after I'd told him my story. He welcomed me in and served me a great feast, promising to purify me on one condition: that I would fight to protect Troy if it was ever in danger. I agreed immediately.

> Priam welcomed me in and served me a great feast, promising to purify me on one condition: that I would fight to protect Troy if it was ever in danger. I agreed immediately.

Once the ritual was over, I returned to Thermodon and became queen of the Amazons. It was not an easy job but I was happy to be busy. Every morning began with training. I led my women in runs and marches across the hills, taught them to shoot arrows at moving targets from horseback and encouraged them to fight longer, harder, and more fearlessly than they believed they could.

In the afternoons I sent out hunting parties and oversaw the worship of our patron gods: my father, the war-god Ares, and Artemis, goddess of hunting and the wild. In the evenings I would gather all the women together to build a bonfire and feast. No matter how late we stayed up laughing and practicing our battle dances, we would be up again at dawn to train.

One night a strange man appeared in Thermodon, wearing a traveler's cloak covered in the dust of a long journey. The watch-women drew their bows, ready for a fight. "No need for that!" I hollered, gesturing for them to down their weapons.

"I think this man is a messenger. We must hear him out."

"Greetings, warrior-souled Penthesilea," the messenger declared, dropping to his knees before me. "I have been sent by King Priam. The Greeks have invaded with a fleet of more than a thousand ships and an army of a hundred-thousand men. Our greatest warrior, horse-taming Hector, has been slain and Troy is in danger. Priam begs you not to forget your old friendship and promises now he and his kingdom are in danger. He needs your help."

> "Priam begs you not to forget your old friendship and promises now he and his kingdom are in danger. He needs your help."

This was the moment my soldiers and I had been preparing for. I chose twelve of my best fighters and asked one of my sisters to rule over the Amazons while I was gone. I knew that she would make sure everyone was looked after, even if I never returned. Then we collected our armor and our weapons, saddled our horses, and made our way to Troy.

From far away, Troy looks the same as it did when I was last here years ago. The citadel sits on a hill above the plains below and its gold-topped towers are protected by sturdy battlements. It's only when we ride closer that we begin to see the signs of war. Smoke rises from the Greek encampment down on the beach and vultures swoop low over the battlefield. The streets of houses built on the slopes leading to the city are shuttered and deserted; all the people have clearly fled to the safety of the walled city. The great city gates are locked and barred, and we have to tell the password to four different guards before we're allowed inside.

> "You were the only person I could think of," Priam says, "who might be able to inspire them to be brave again."

We're escorted straight up to the palace and shown into Priam's throne hall. He greets me like a long-lost daughter and begins to tell us about the war. Things have been going badly since Hector's death and his troops are losing morale. "You were the only person I could think of," he says, "who might be able to inspire them to be brave again."

That night we feast and discuss our tactics; we'll corner the Greeks tomorrow, with me and my twelve warriors leading the charge. Priam asks if he should have us shown to our rooms but I refuse—my women and I prefer to camp.

The next morning dawns, and I gather my women around me. I check the buckles of their breastplates and the straps of their half-moon-shaped shields. I count out a stock of arrows for each warrior and inspect the sharpness of our fearsome double-headed battle axes. We go over the plans we've practiced together time and time again. Everything is ready.

I throw my cloak over my chainmail, clear my throat, and address my troops. "Comrades, I'll keep this speech short— we've got Greeks to kill. You are the best of the best, so let's show the men exactly what we women are made of!"

The Protective Witch-Queen

Circe

You may have heard of me—if you have, I should assure you that you have nothing to fear.

They say that my cunning and skill makes me a danger to men, but they just don't understand the reasons for my actions.

I have responsibilities—to my people as a ruler and to nature as a witch—and those responsibilities will **always** come first.

I was born the daughter of Helios, god of the sun, and a sea-nymph named Perse. I grew up in the eastern land of Colchis, where my brother Aeetes was king. He was a harsh ruler with a temper like fire, who guarded his kingdom and his treasure so jealously that he tried to kill any foreigner who dared set foot on Colchian soil. When I asked him why, he just grimaced and said that our father would give me a kingdom of my own when I was grown up, and that I'd understand then.

In Colchis, I was given an education fit for a queen—no, for a *goddess*. I learned to weave the finest cloth, to sing the sweetest songs, and to run my own household. But the most important skill I was taught was magic.

I've always found it strange how stories speak of magic as though it's a gift, received fully formed and at random. Magic is a skill—an *art*. You need talent, of course, but that's not enough. The most powerful witches are the ones who practice. And I did. I spent my days in the woods, learning the names and properties of flowers and herbs. I spent my evenings seeing to the rituals of the witch-goddess Hecate or poring over potion recipes and incantations.

> Magic is a skill—an art. You need talent, of course, but that's not enough. The most powerful witches are the ones who practice.

The day I came of age, my father's chariot landed in the courtyard. It was covered in hammered gold and deep-red rubies studded the spokes of the wheels. Harnessed to it were four pure-white horses with wide, feathered wings. They'd have looked as serene and harmless as doves if it hadn't been for the plumes of fire shooting from their nostrils. My father had come to take me to my own kingdom—a little island in the far west of the world.

I watched the landscape change and change again as my father drove the chariot across the sky. We soared over the highest mountains and lowest valleys, the ever-flowing rivers and seas, and the cities and villages of the world. My father tugged at the reins and the horses reared around, circling a small island called Aeaea. High hills rose up behind

the beaches and natural harbors that surrounded the edges of the island. At its center was a valley, dipped down and sheltered. The whole island was covered with a rich forest of oak and pine; it was perfect.

"Look after this land, and everything that dwells on it," my father warned as he helped me down from the chariot. "Whatever that takes."

For the next few months, I worked from dawn until midnight. My first task was to learn the lay of the land. I walked the island until I knew every hill and cove, every clearing and cave, every pool and stream. My second was to win the trust of my new people. Aeaea was populated only with women. They were nymphs—nature goddesses connected to the trees and streams of the island—and the sweetest, gentlest beings I ever met. My third task was to get to know the wildlife of the island. Each day I went exploring in the woods until I'd catalogued every plant and could greet every animal by name.

Finally, I found a natural clearing, sheltered in the crook of the valley near a fresh spring, and built a palace for my nymphs and I to live in. It had airy halls and warm fires, comfy bedrooms and a laboratory for potion making. Fountains trickled in the courtyards and friendly lions and bears played on the lawns outside.

"Look after this land, and everything that dwells on it," my father warned as he helped me down from the chariot. "Whatever that takes."

I've been here so long now that I know Aeaea like the back of my hand, which means I know immediately if anything is out of place. One day a stag, a proud creature by the name of Irenaeus, is killed; and later on I find two trees felled in the western woods. That night I decide to climb up to the roof-terrace I use for growing herbs and see a thin curl of smoke twisting up across the moon. It looks like it is coming from one of the beaches—there must be strangers on the island.

I don't want my nymphs to be afraid, so I check the bolts on the doors and try to go back to bed. I hope that if the winds change, whoever it was might be gone in the morning.

The next day I work hard to pretend everything is normal. I am weaving in the great hall when I hear the low growl of voices coming from the portico outside. Looking out, I see a group of men.

I desperately want to be a more welcoming ruler than my brother was, so I decide to give these strangers the benefit of the doubt. I fling open the polished double doors and invite them inside. They look cold, and hungry, and terrified.

I sit my visitors down by the fire on my most comfortable high-backed chairs, sending one nymph to get them stools to rest their feet on and asking another to ready the room for a feast. As nymphs stream into the hall carrying silver tables that they lay with golden cups and bowls, the vine-nymph Melite begins to mix the wine and I slip off to the kitchens to   prepare the food.

Not twenty minutes have passed before I hear crashing and shouting. Dropping everything, I run back through the colonnades to the great hall. I peek around the corner of the archway. The room is in chaos—the men are ordering the women around, demanding more food and wine. One of my guests is tormenting a lion who was just trying to lie peacefully by the fire, while another has broken the lock on one of my chests and is rifling through the items inside.

I am enraged. I run back through the kitchens to my potion room. I pass the racks of drying herbs

and the shelves of ointment jars until I reach the small, locked cupboard at the back. I grab the vial I am looking for and rush back into the kitchen. I pull out the cork and pour the pink liquid into a golden cauldron, mixing it with honey, wine, milk, and meal until I know the men won't be able to taste the potion.

I carry the sweet drink into the hall and offer it to each of the men in turn. They take it without thanking me and guzzle it down. *Greedy pigs.*

Once every man is served, I sit back on my throne by the fire and watch. A man named Polites is the first to go. He starts snuffling and snorting, thick hair grows from his skin, his legs get shorter and his body wider. Finally a small, curly pink tail sprouts from his behind. The other men begin to panic but it is too late. Before long the hall is filled with angry little pigs.

"Grunt as much as you like," I say to piggy-Polites as I shoo the men outside to the pigsty. "You made your bed when you disrespected me, this island, and these women. Now you'll have to lie in it." I chuck them some acorns to snack on—I'm not a *monster.*

A few hours pass and the nymphs and I are enjoying ourselves singing songs and finishing up our feast. The peace is broken by a rapping at the great doors. A man appears—a late arrival, I assume, from the same crew as my new pigs.

"You made your bed when you disrespected me, this island, and these women," I said. "Now you'll have to lie in it."

I offer him a seat and fetch a glass of the sweetened potion. I wait. Nothing happens. I offer him a second. Again nothing. I don't understand; I've never met a mortal who is immune to magic.

"Are you surprised," he asks, raising an eyebrow, "that I'm still human?"

So, he knows what happened to his friends . . . A picture of events quickly begins to form in my head. I'm determined to get to the bottom of it.

"Have you taken an antidote to my potion?" I ask. "Was it the black-rooted, white-flowered herb moly?"

He nods.

"A herb far too dangerous for mortals to pluck, which means it *must* have been given to you by a god—which one?"

He says nothing.

"Was it Hermes?" I can tell by his expression I'm right. I sigh; that god is *nothing* but

trouble. "And why, I wonder, would Hermes care if you were man or pig . . . Who are you? Where do you come from? Where were you born? Who are your parents?"

He's about to respond when I put it all together.

"You must be Odysseus."

He starts in shock.

"How . . . how do you . . ."

I stand up and pour us

both some non-enchanted wine. Odyssesus is said to be the cleverest man in Greece so I'm curious to hear his story. "Hermes told me to expect you at some point. You must be on your way back from the war at Troy, I suppose? Stop a while and tell me about your journey."

Odysseus shakes his head. "Surely you can hardly expect me to sit and drink wine with you while you hold my men captive?"

"Your men are held captive here because of *their* actions. I have responsibilities as a ruler to protect my people and my land."

"You do. So, you must understand that I too have a responsibility to protect my men."

I think for a moment, then I offer him a deal. "I will free your men on two conditions: that they apologize to my nymphs and that you guarantee that for as long as you stay on Aeaea they will do *nothing* further to harm the island."

"It's a deal."

We shake on it. I find the reversal ointment from my storeroom and smear it on each pig's snout. One by one they transform back into men— grateful and apologetic ones!

What happened next?

The eight women you met in this book did remarkable things, and you've had an insight into an epic moment in their story. After we left them, some went on to win the power, happiness, and respect they were looking for, but others weren't so fortunate. The world of Greek mythology, after all, could be an unpredictable and dangerous place.

Pandora

In the beginning, only the gods had access to fire. And so when Prometheus (Epimetheus' brother) stole it and gave it to humans, he made the god Zeus very angry. Zeus decided to punish humanity. He knew that Pandora would be curious enough to open the jar he had filled with evils—that was why he created her in the first place. But Pandora's quick thinking in closing the jar saved Hope—the state of mind which helps people deal with the difficult parts of life. Pandora went on to have a daughter with Epimetheus. This was the first human child ever born and she was named Pyrrha, which means fire.

Medusa

After her transformation, Medusa became one of the most famous and feared beings in all of Greece. A young hero named Perseus was sent on a fatal mission to kill her and bring her head to King Polydectes of Seriphos. It was a quest Perseus could only achieve using magical winged sandals and an invisibility helmet. He crept up on Medusa, watching her reflection in his shield so that he wouldn't be turned to stone, and cut off her head. Euryale and Sthenno pursued Perseus for miles, trying to avenge their sister, but he got away. When Medusa was beheaded, two magical creatures sprung from her body—the giant Khrysaor and the winged-horse Pegasus.

Medea

When Medea and Jason were fleeing Colchis, they were pursued by
her father's ships. She decided to kill her brother, chop him up, and
throw his body parts in the sea, so her father would slow down as he
tried to collect them. She and Jason settled in Corinth and had children.
For ten years they lived happily. Medea used her arts to end a famine
in the city and even turned down the advances of the god Zeus. But
then Jason's ambitions grew, and he decided to leave Medea and marry
the daughter of Corinth's king. Some sources say Medea was so upset
that she murdered Jason's fiancée with a poisoned wedding gown,
before killing her and Jason's children to punish him. Other sources say
Medea hid her children in the Temple of Hera, where they either died
accidentally or were killed by the angry Corinthians. Medea later flew to
Athens—in a golden chariot driven by dragons—where she married the
king and had another son.

Atalanta

Although the first major event in Greek mythology where Atalanta appears is the Calydonian boar hunt, Atalanta had other adventures, too. Some sources say she was one of the heroes who joined Jason's quest to find the Golden Fleece. She and Hippomenes went on to have a son named Parthenopaeus who became one of the "Seven against Thebes": seven leaders whose army took back the throne of the kingdom of Thebes which had been stolen from its owner. Hippomenes, however, made a fatal error. He never thanked Aphrodite for all the help she had given him in his quest to win Atalanta, and so she tricked him and Atalanta into disrespecting the gods who promptly transformed them both into lions.

Ariadne

Ariadne saved Theseus and his fellow Athenian victims from the Minotaur, but did that make him grateful? *No.* Theseus stopped his ship at an island to replenish his supplies and then abandoned Ariadne as she slept. At first, she was heartbroken, but it turned out to be a blessing in disguise. The wine god Dionysus visited the island in his tiger-drawn chariot. They fell in love and married. Ariadne was transformed into a goddess and Dionysus made her crown into a constellation of stars as a token of his love for her.

Helen

When Menelaus returned to Sparta and discovered Helen was missing, he was outraged. He called upon the other suitors who had made the oath to come to his aid. Together, they assembled a fleet of one thousand ships and sailed for Troy. The Trojan War raged for ten long years and saw countless heroes, including Penthesilea, killed. When it was over, Menelaus decided to kill Helen—until she stood before him and made a speech in her own defense. She argued her case so eloquently that Menelaus forgave her. They returned to Sparta where they lived as husband and wife and ruled their kingdom together.

Penthesilea

Penthesilea was a brave and expert warrior—but not an invincible one. When she and her warrior women rushed into battle during the Trojan War, Penthesilea slew hero after hero. Just as the Greeks were turning to flee, Achilles, the greatest of all the Greek heroes, arrived. The two fought long and hard but eventually it was Achilles who won out. As Penthesilea was dying, Achilles began to regret what he had done. This woman was the bravest and best warrior he had ever seen. He demanded the Greeks treat her with respect and returned her body to the Trojans to be given a hero's burial.

Circe

After Circe agreed to reverse the pig spell, Odysseus and his men stayed and lived with her on Aeaea for a full year. She and Odysseus fell in love and had a son together. But Odysseus and his crew had a homeland named Ithaca to return to, and Circe had an island to rule. The Odyssey (the name of Odysseus' ten-year long journey home) was full of dangers and Circe's parting advice saved Odysseus' life. She taught him the magical secrets of how to contact the spirits of the underworld and sent him to speak to a dead prophet named Tiresias, who would tell him how to make it home alive.

Bibliography

Primary Sources

Aelian, *Historical Miscellany.*

Apollonius of Rhodes, *Argonautica.*

Callimachus, *Hymns.*

Diodorus Siculus, *Library of History.*

Euripides, *Medea.*

Euripides, *The Trojan Women.*

Gaius Valerius Flaccus, *Argonautica.*

Hesiod, *Catalogue of Women.*

Hesiod, *Theogony.*

Hesiod, *Works and Days.*

Homer, *The Iliad.*

Homer, *The Odyssey.*

Ovid, *Heroides.*

Ovid, *Metamorphoses.*

Pausanias, *Description of Greece.*

Pindar, *Odes.*

Plutarch, *Life of Theseus.*

Pseudo-Apollodorus, *Bibliotheca.*

Pseudo-Hyginus, *Fabulae.*

Quintus Smyrnaeus, *The Fall of Troy.*

Strabo, *Geography.*

Secondary Sources

Graves, Robert. *The Greek Myths.*
London: Penguin, 1955.

Haynes, Natalie. *Pandora's Jar:
Women in the Greek Myths.*
London: Pan Macmillan, 2020.

Hughes, Bettany. *Helen of Troy.*
London: Penguin, 2005.

Man, John. *Amazons.*
London: Bantam Press, 2017.

The author would like to note that alongside printed material, ancient art is also an important resource as the ancient Greeks made sculptures and painted their vases with stories and characters from their myths.

About the author

Honor Cargill-Martin is an author, classicist, and art historian from the United Kingdom. Honor studied Ancient History and Classical Archaeology at the University of Oxford. She won a scholarship and went on to complete a master's in Ancient History. After a second master's in Italian Renaissance art (which featured a lot more Greek myths, just painted this time!), she returned to Oxford to begin a doctorate focusing on ancient Roman history at Christ Church College.

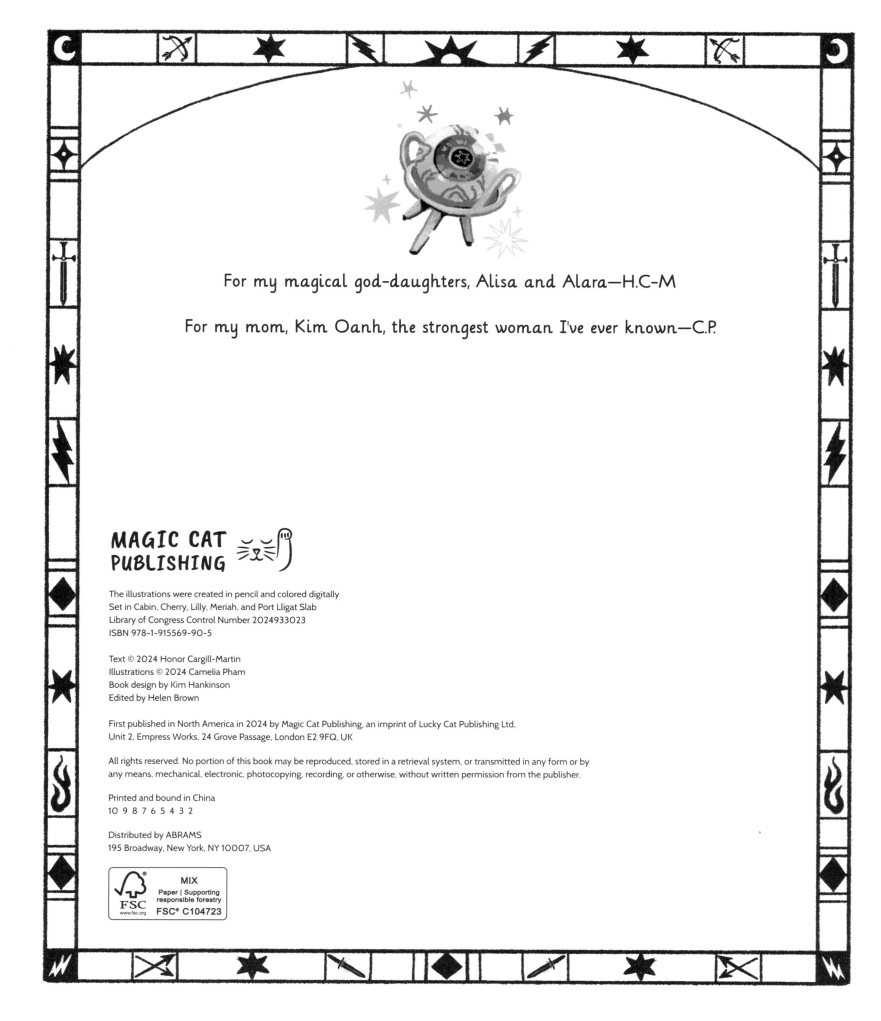

For my magical god-daughters, Alisa and Alara—H.C-M

For my mom, Kim Oanh, the strongest woman I've ever known—C.P.

MAGIC CAT
PUBLISHING

The illustrations were created in pencil and colored digitally
Set in Cabin, Cherry, Lilly, Meriah, and Port Lligat Slab
Library of Congress Control Number 2024933023
ISBN 978-1-915569-90-5

Text © 2024 Honor Cargill-Martin
Illustrations © 2024 Camelia Pham
Book design by Kim Hankinson
Edited by Helen Brown

First published in North America in 2024 by Magic Cat Publishing, an imprint of Lucky Cat Publishing Ltd,
Unit 2, Empress Works, 24 Grove Passage, London E2 9FQ, UK

Printed and bound in China
10 9 8 7 6 5 4 3 2

Distributed by ABRAMS
195 Broadway, New York, NY 10007, USA

FSC
www.fsc.org
MIX
Paper | Supporting
responsible forestry
FSC® C104723

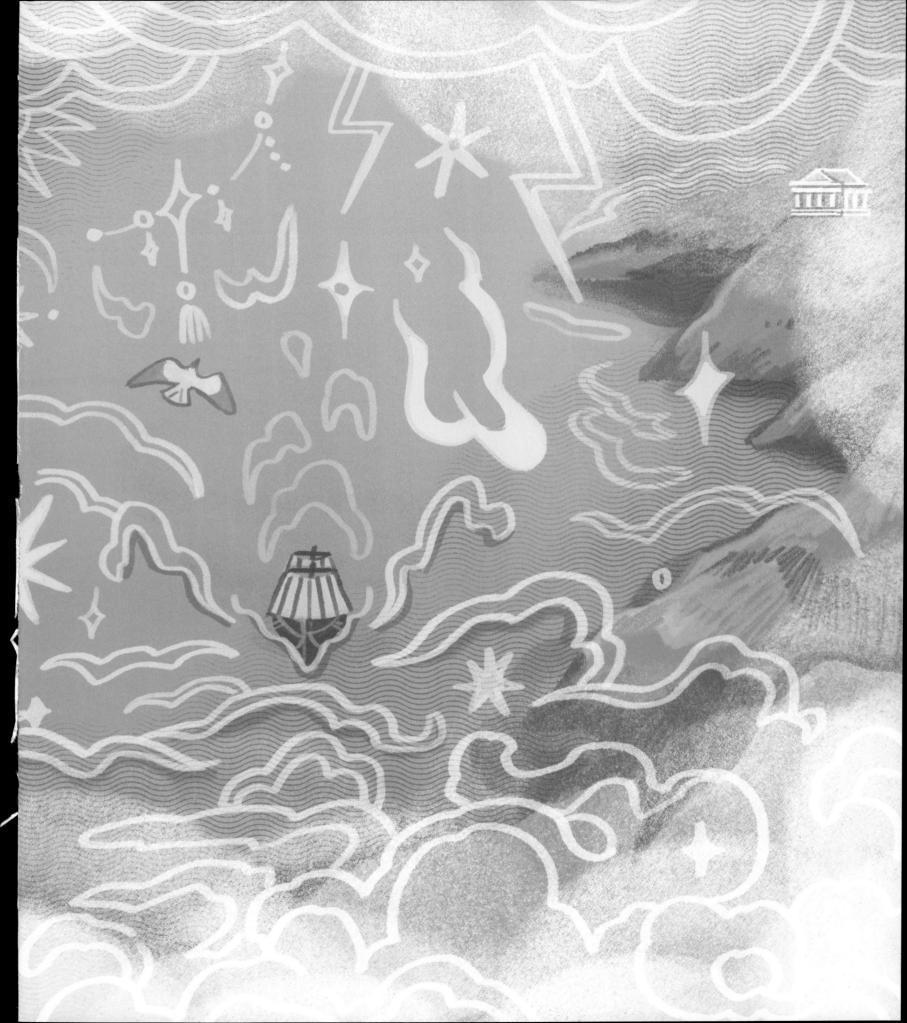

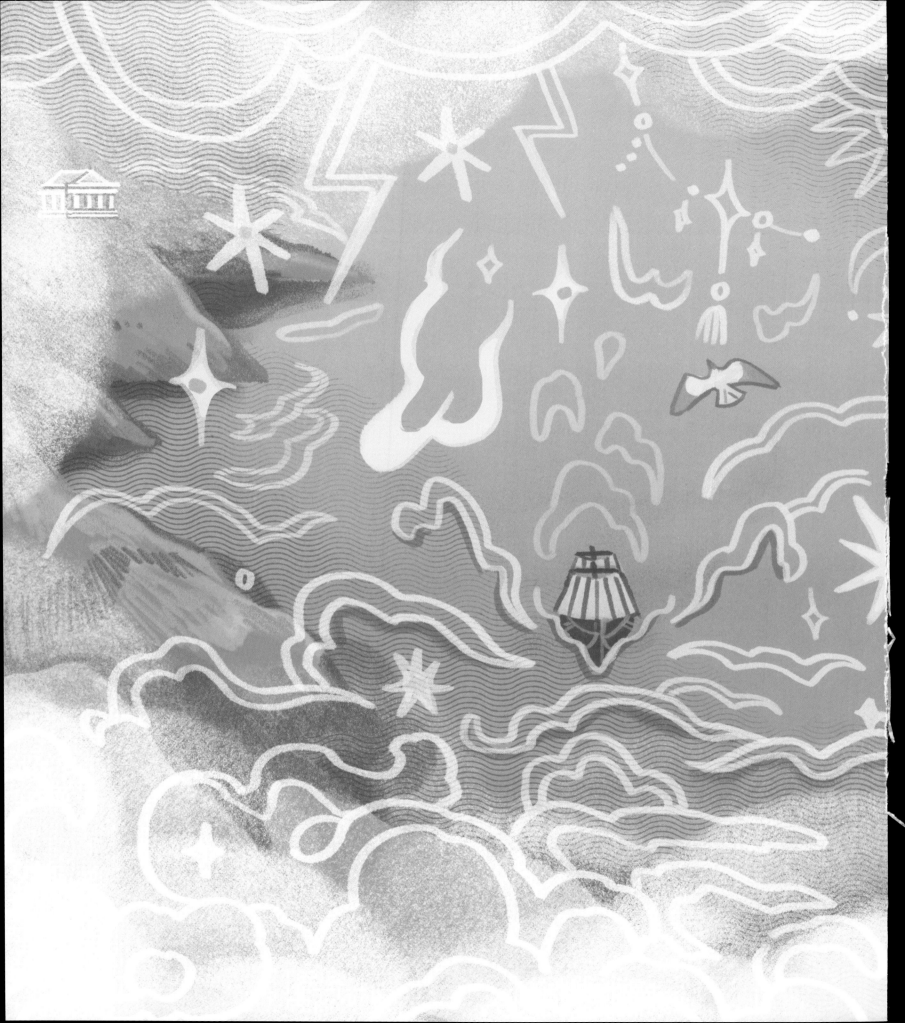

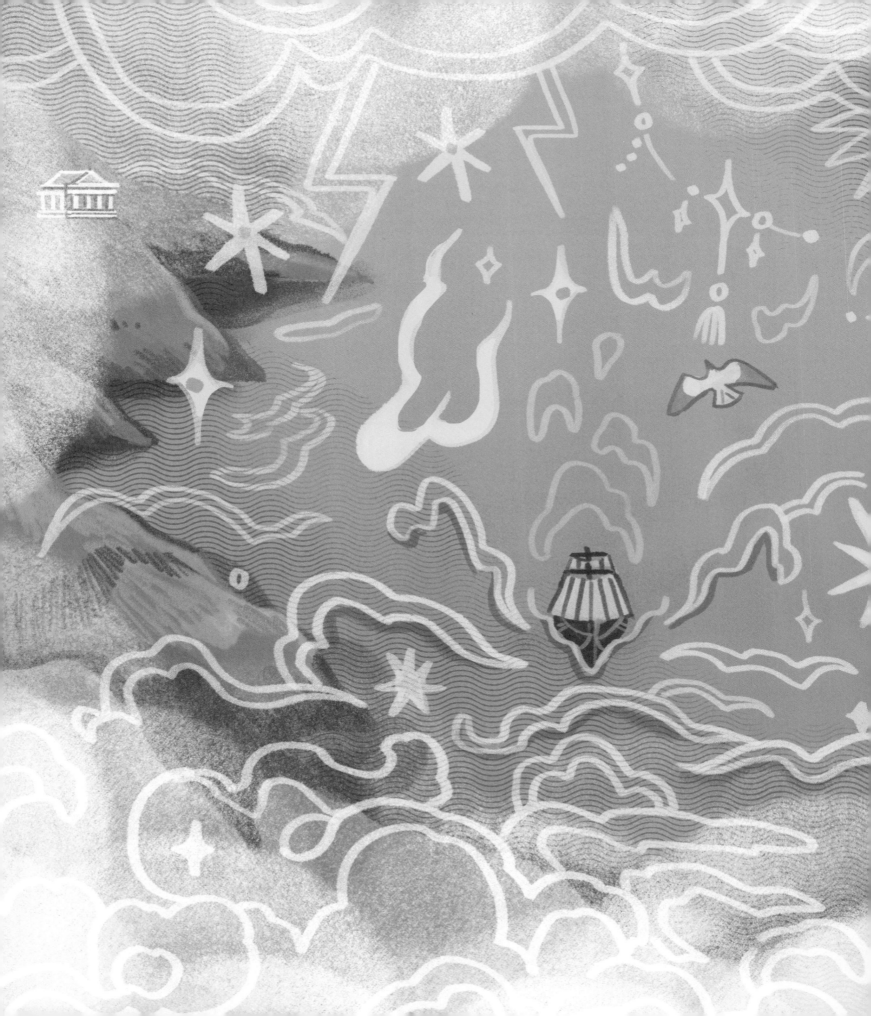